# EXQUISITE Flowers

## coloring Book

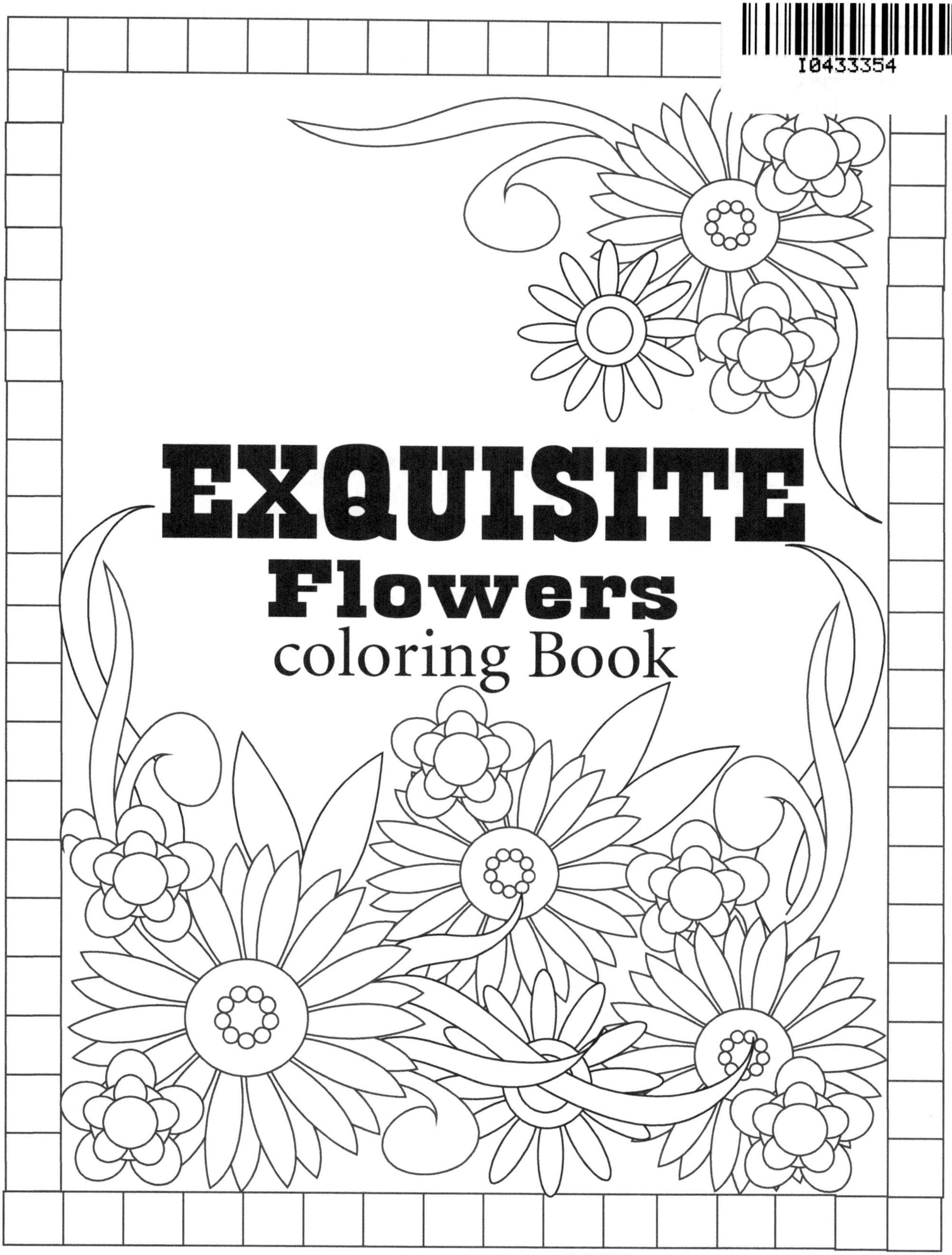

I0433354

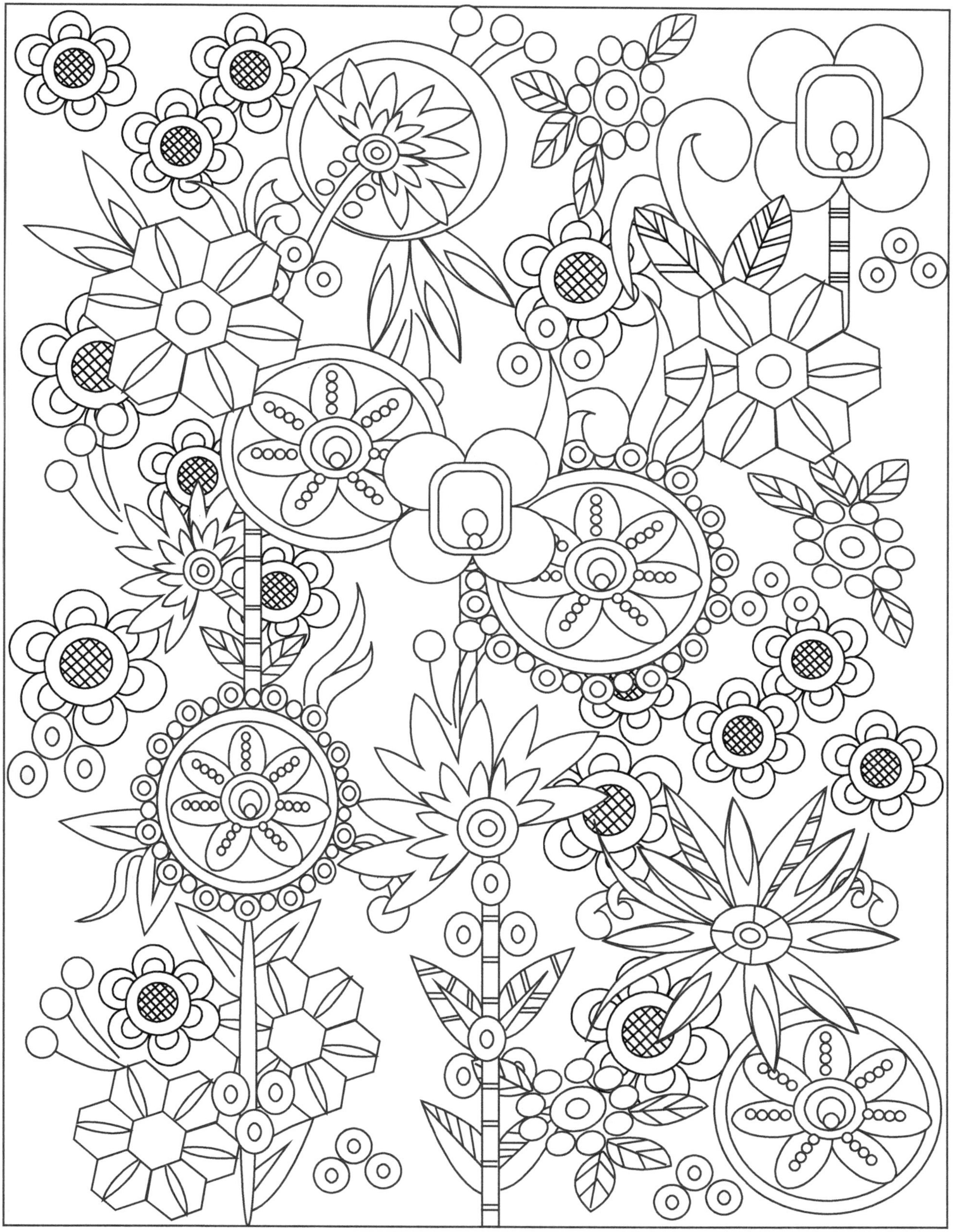

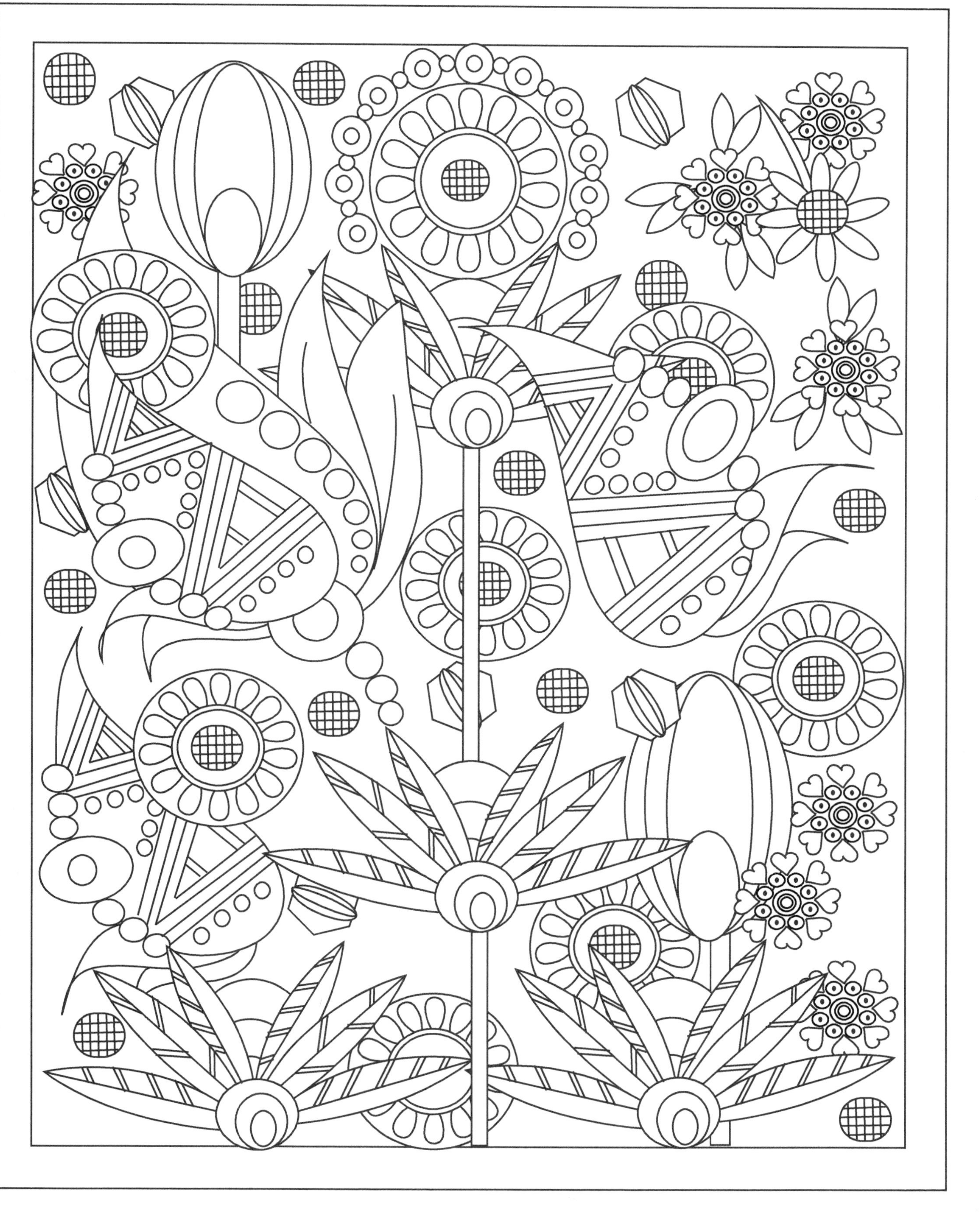

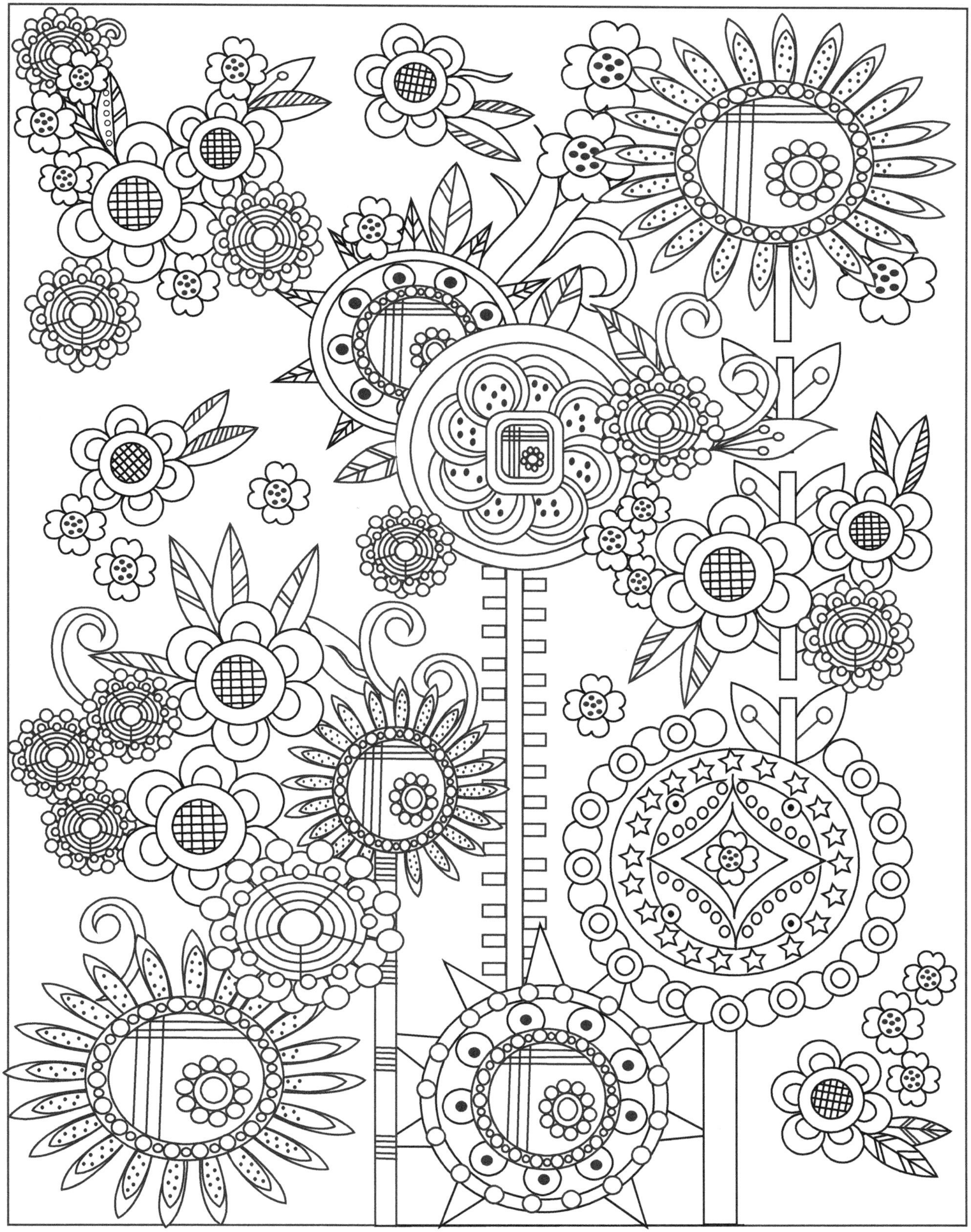

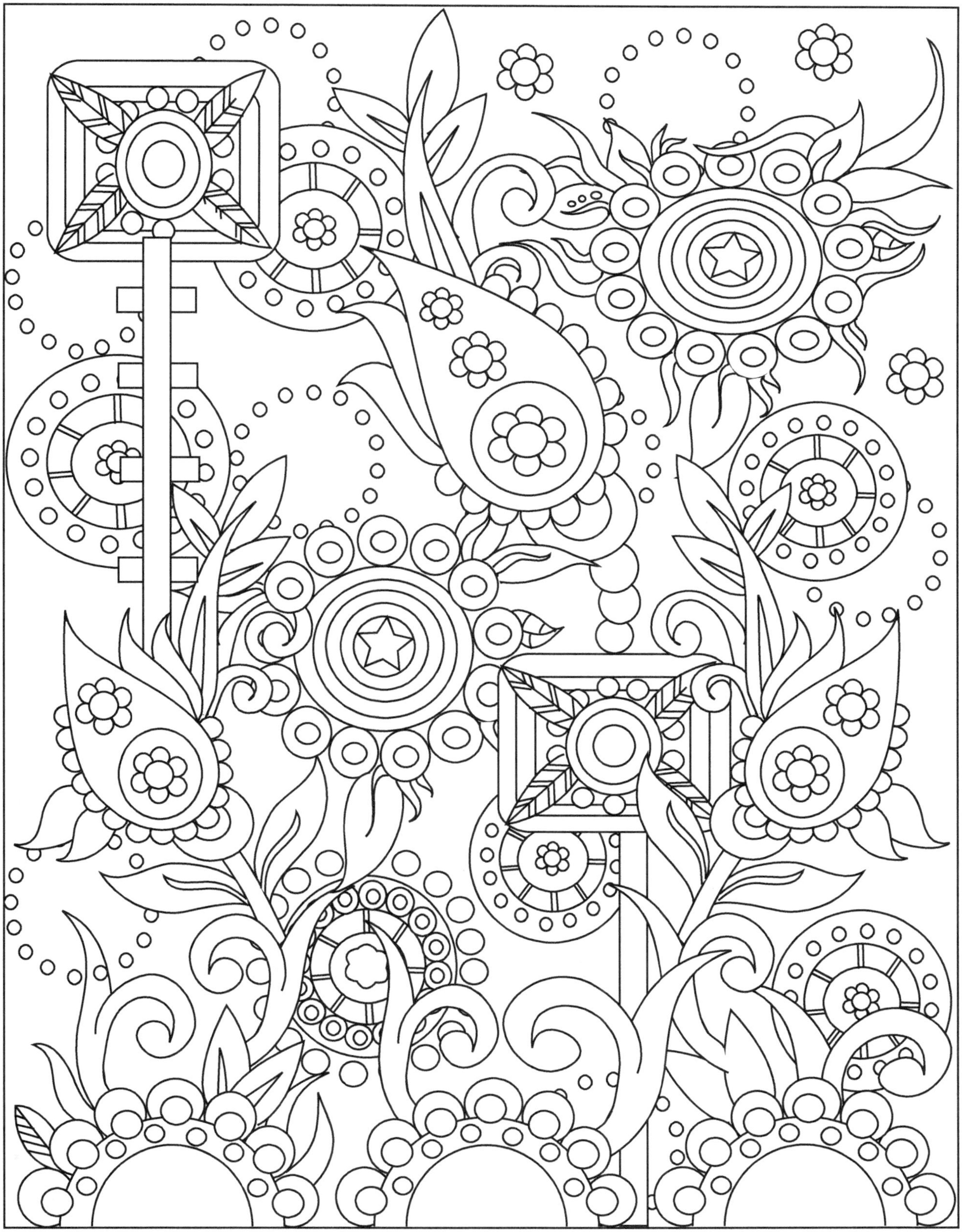

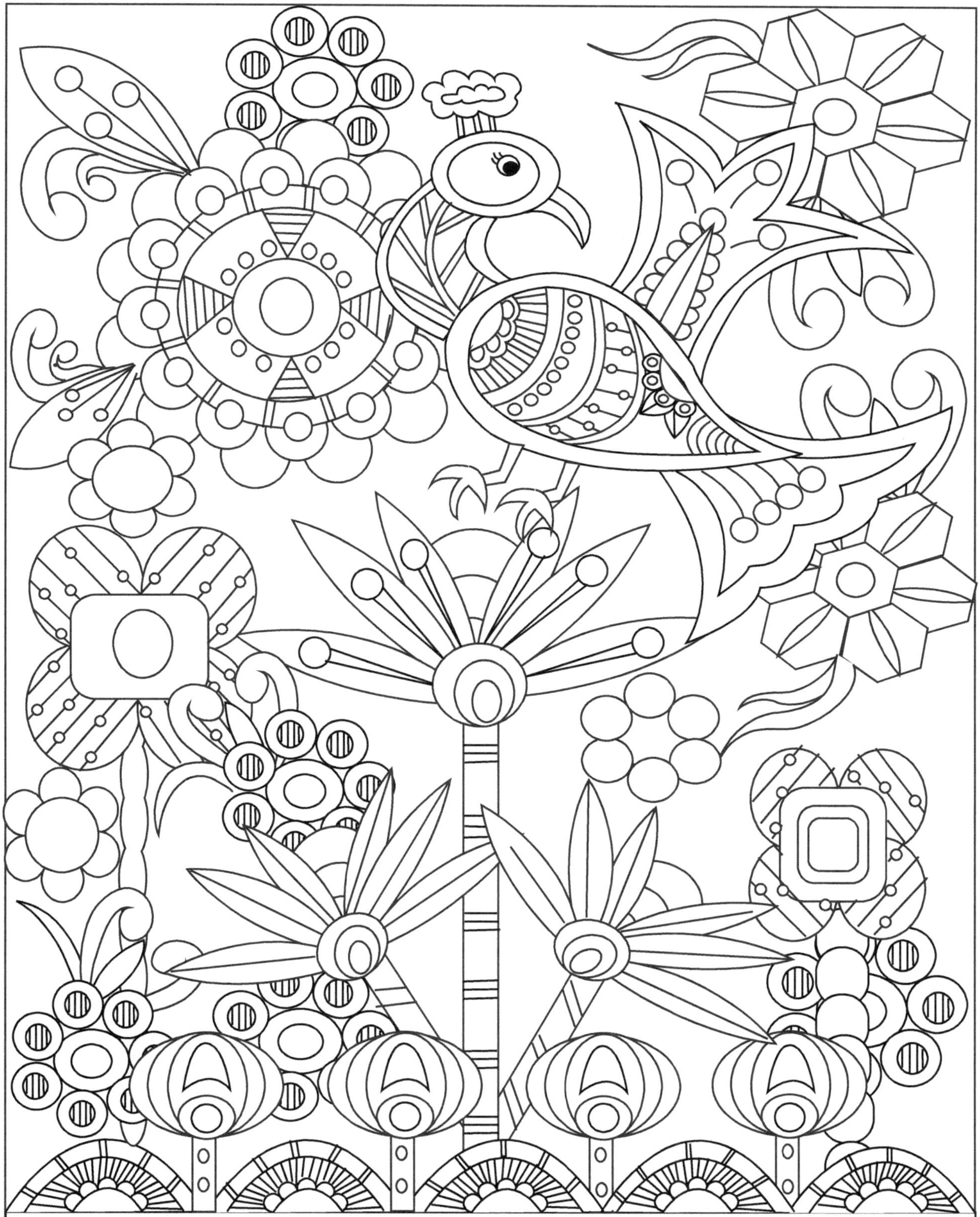

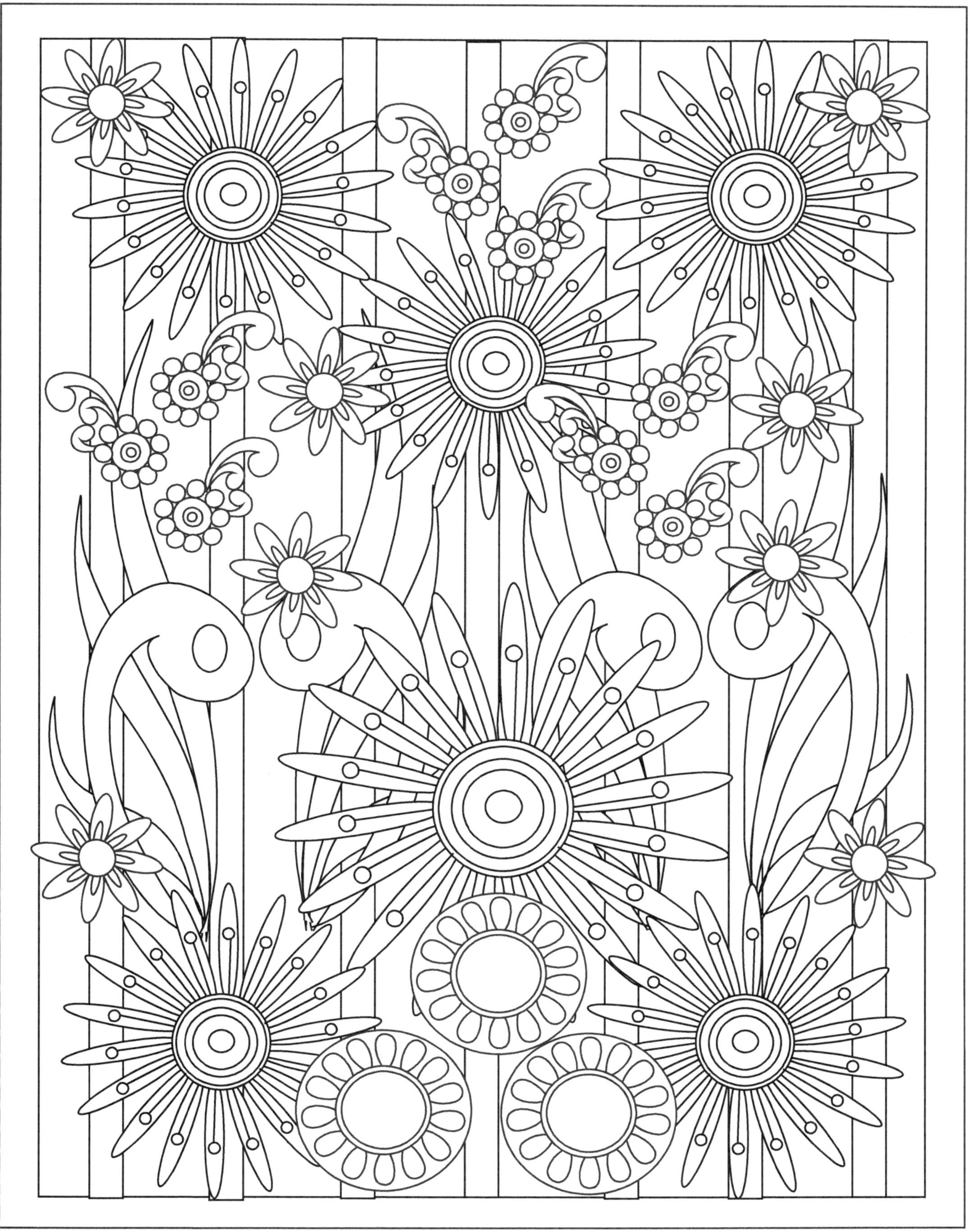

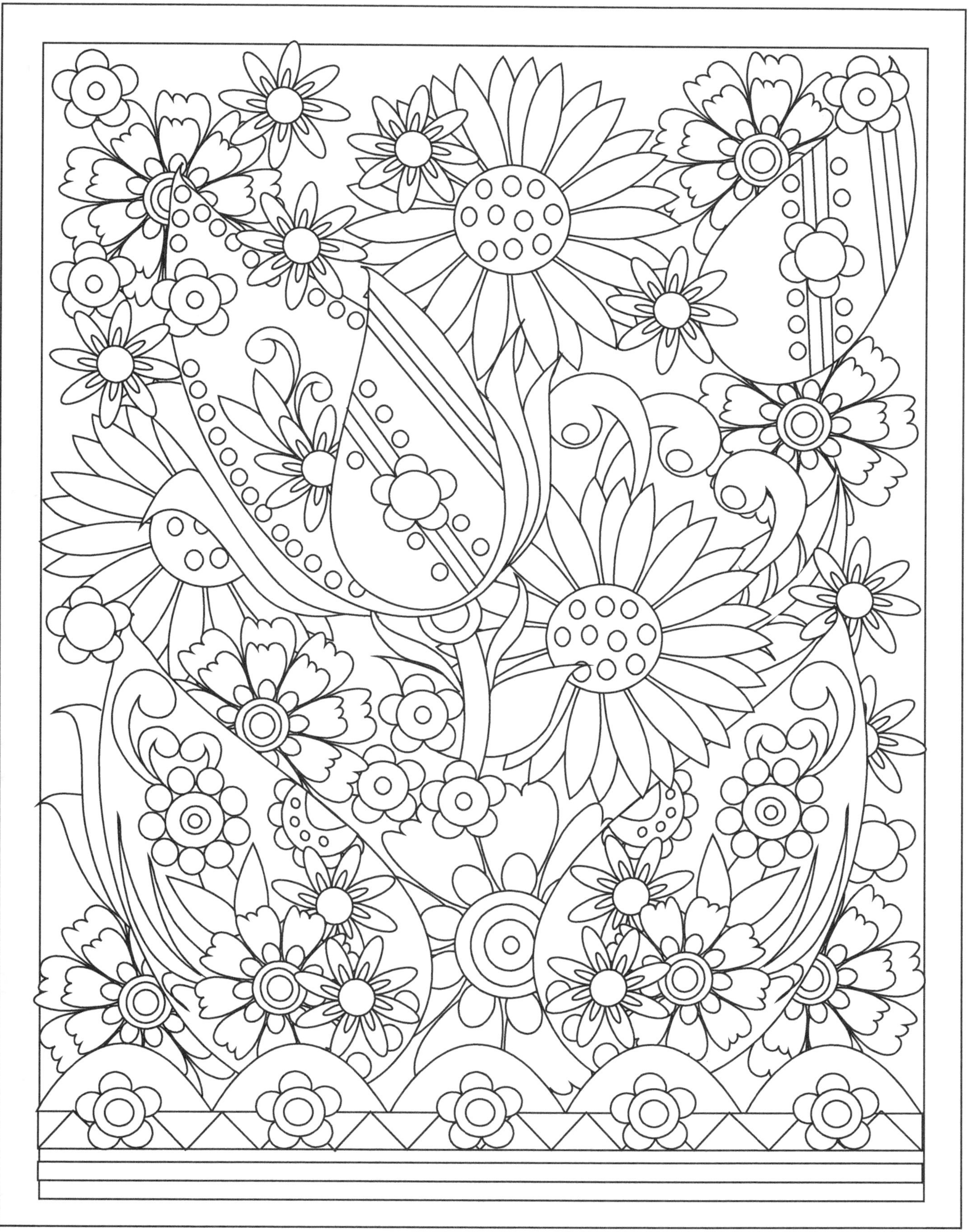

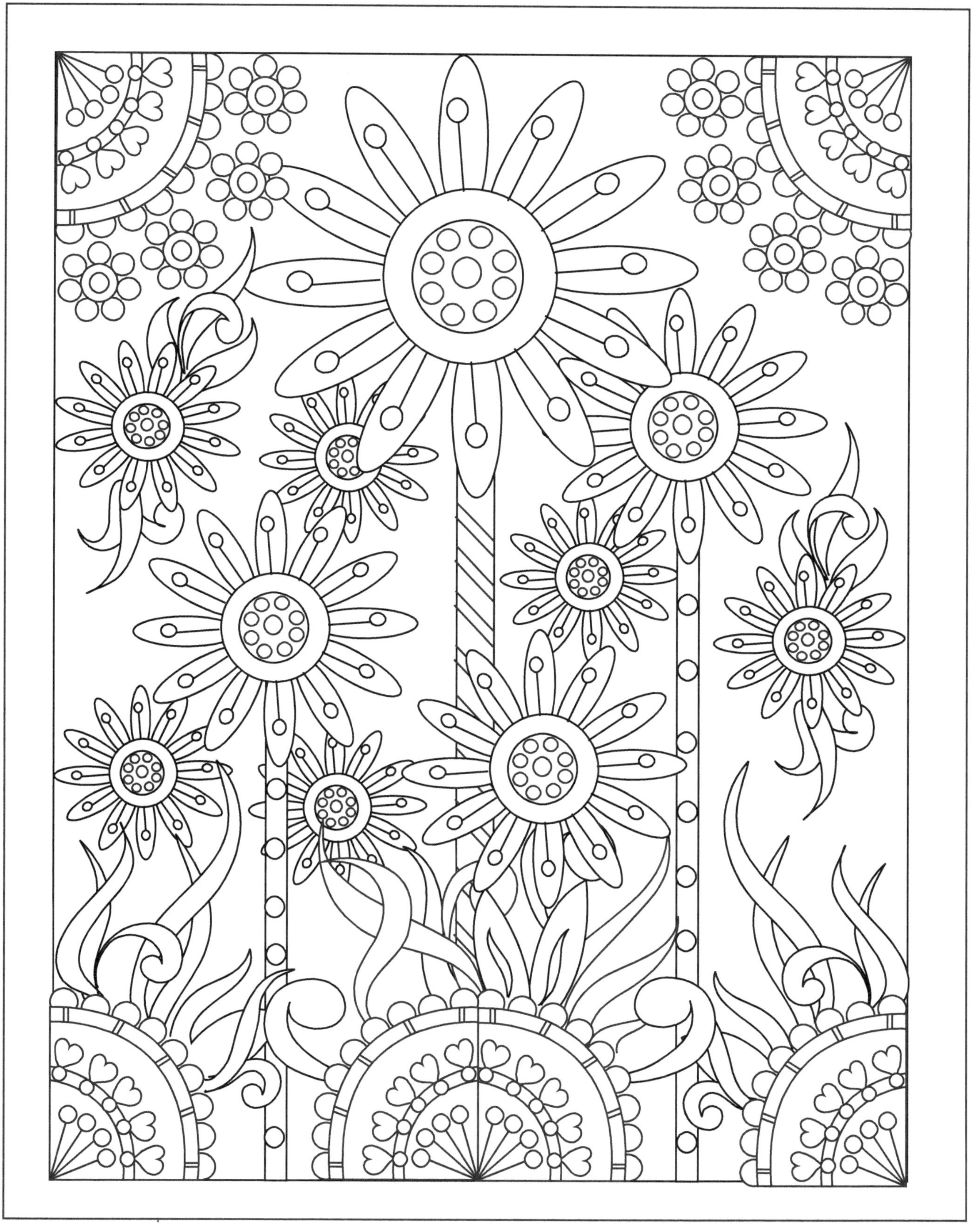

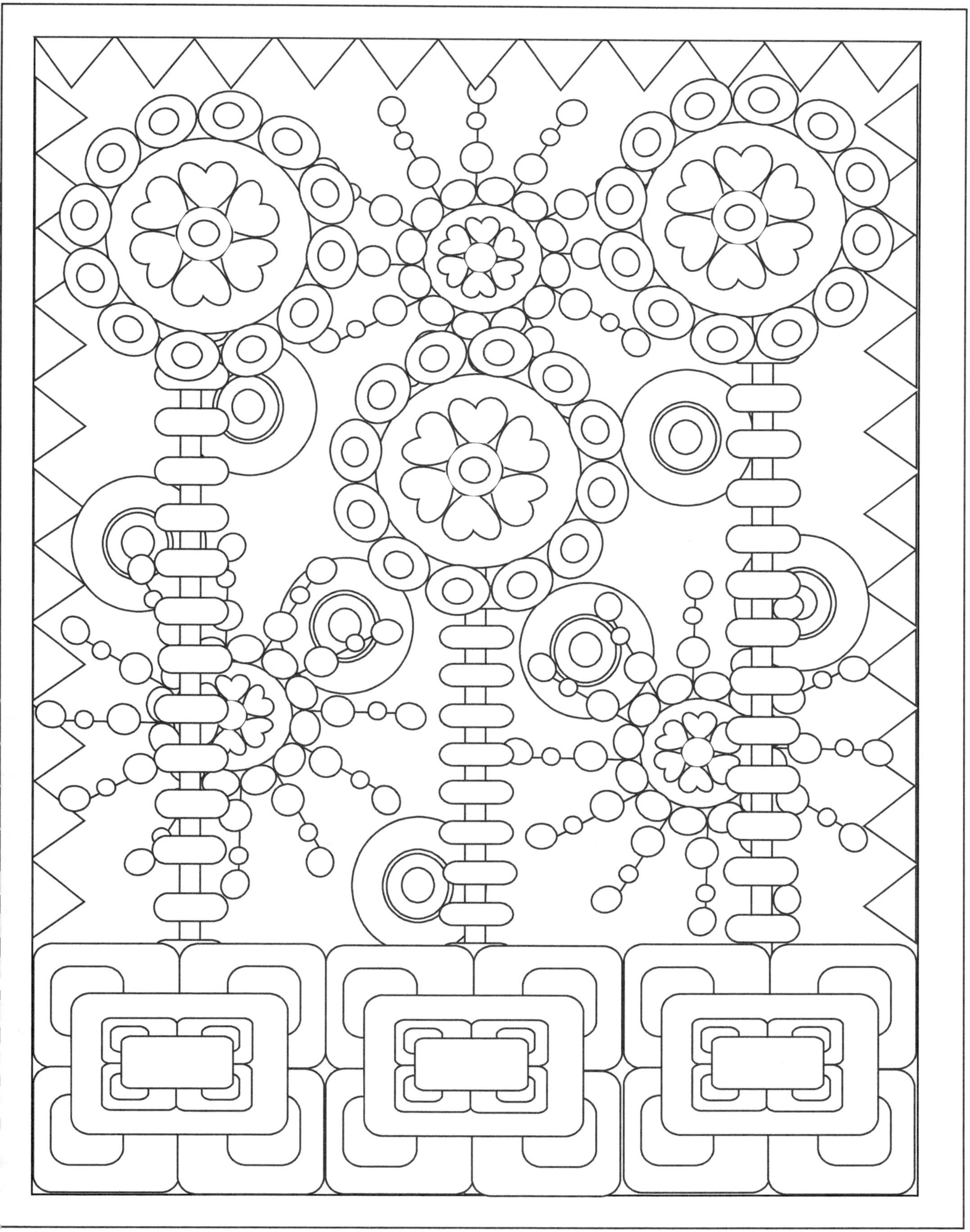

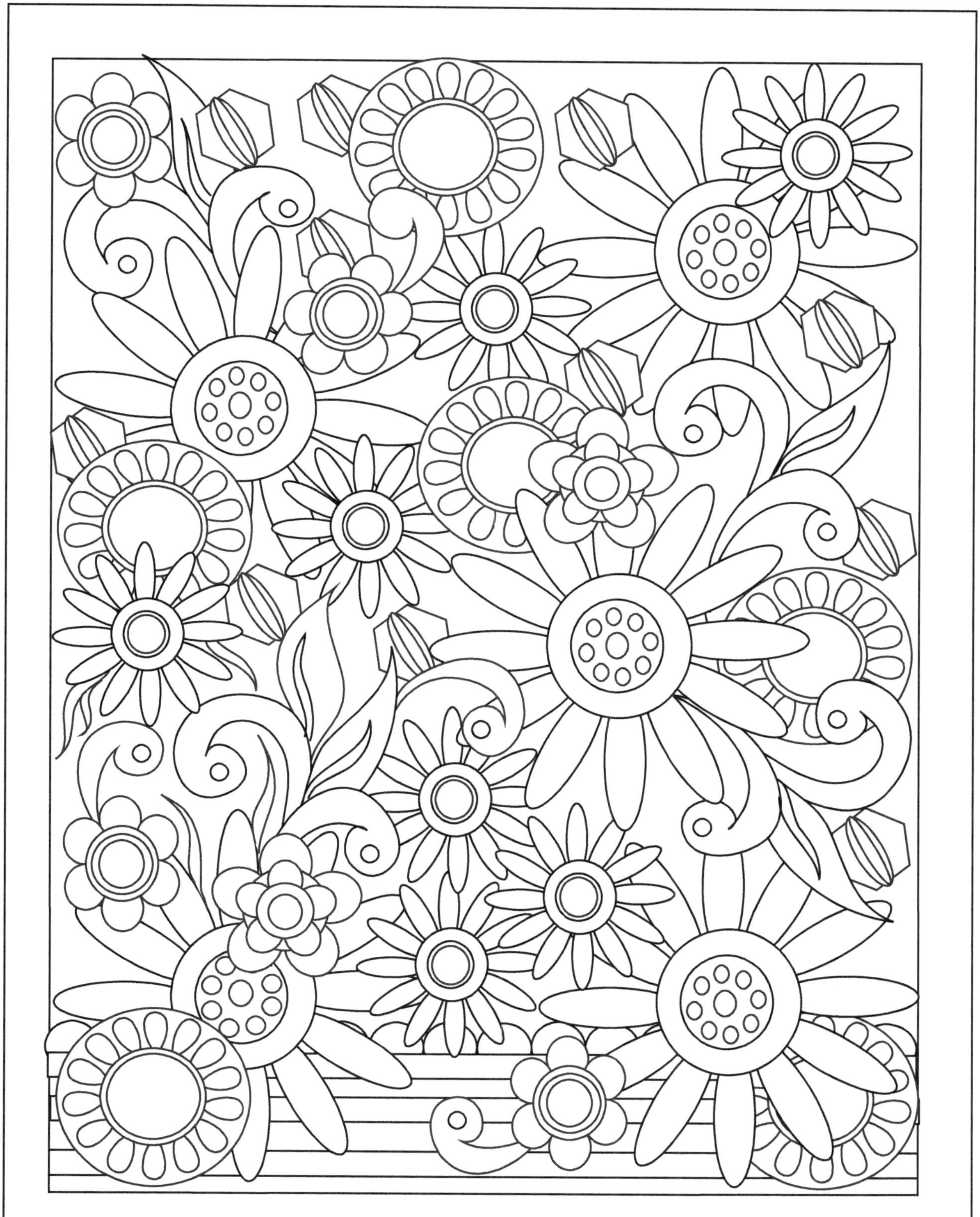

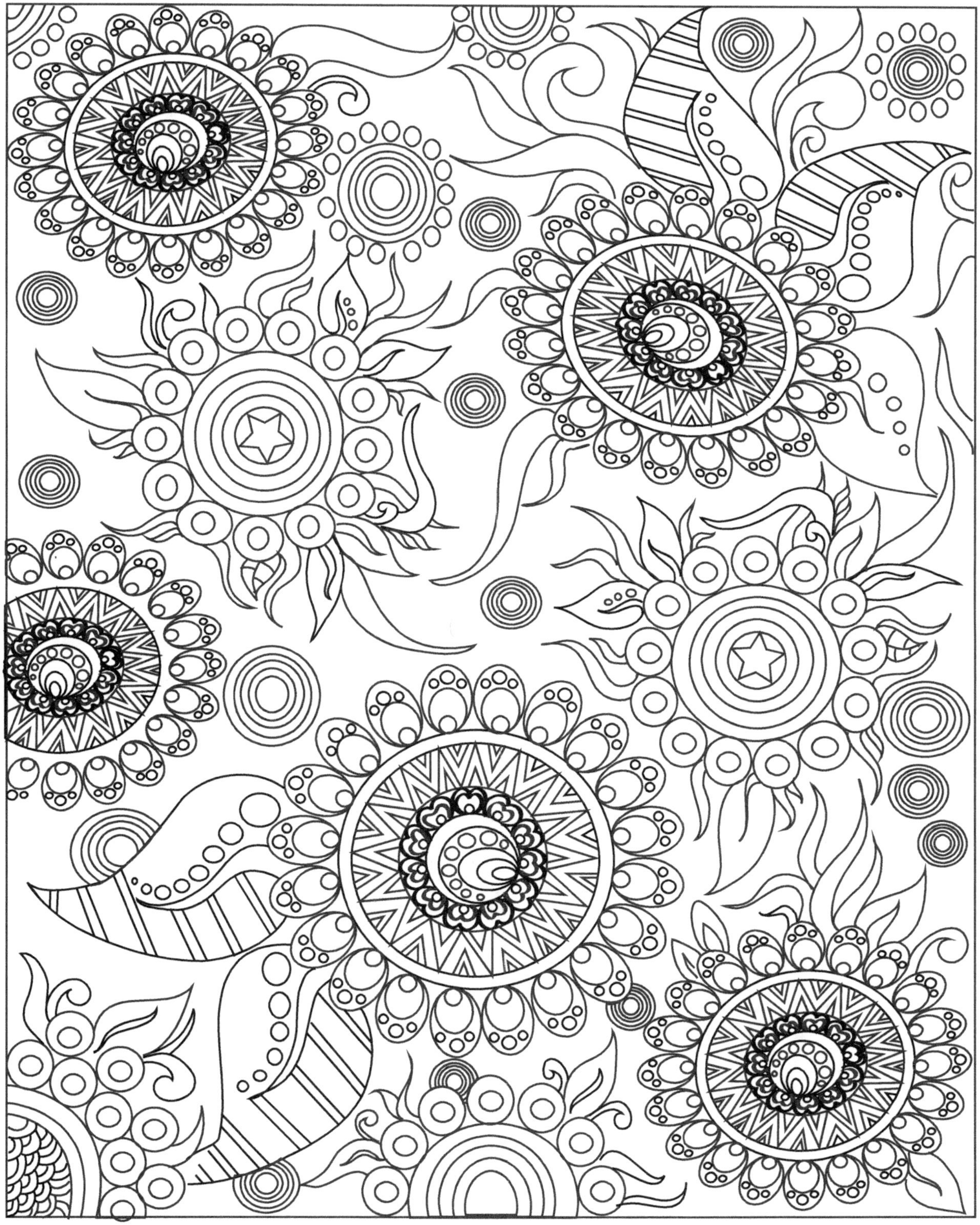

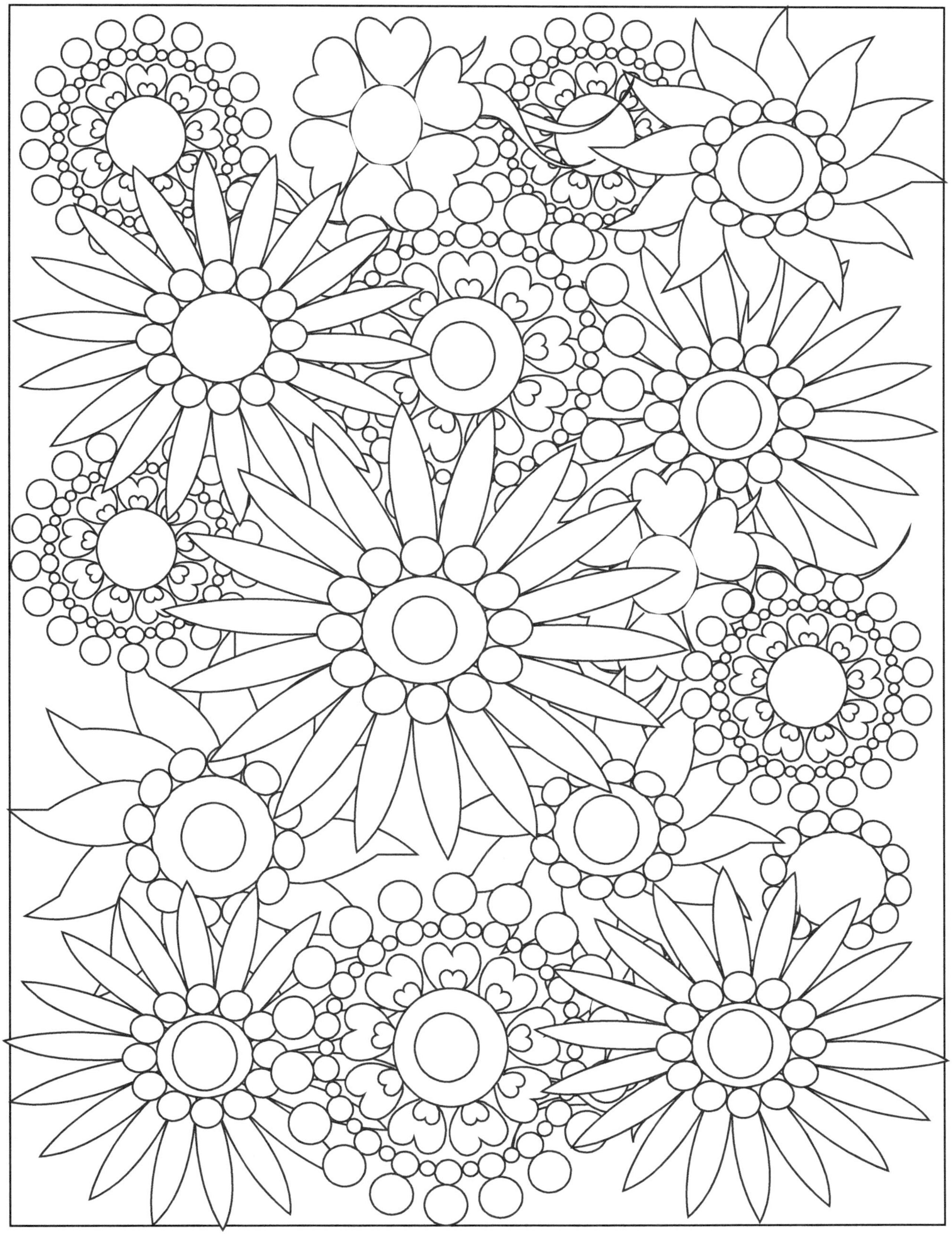

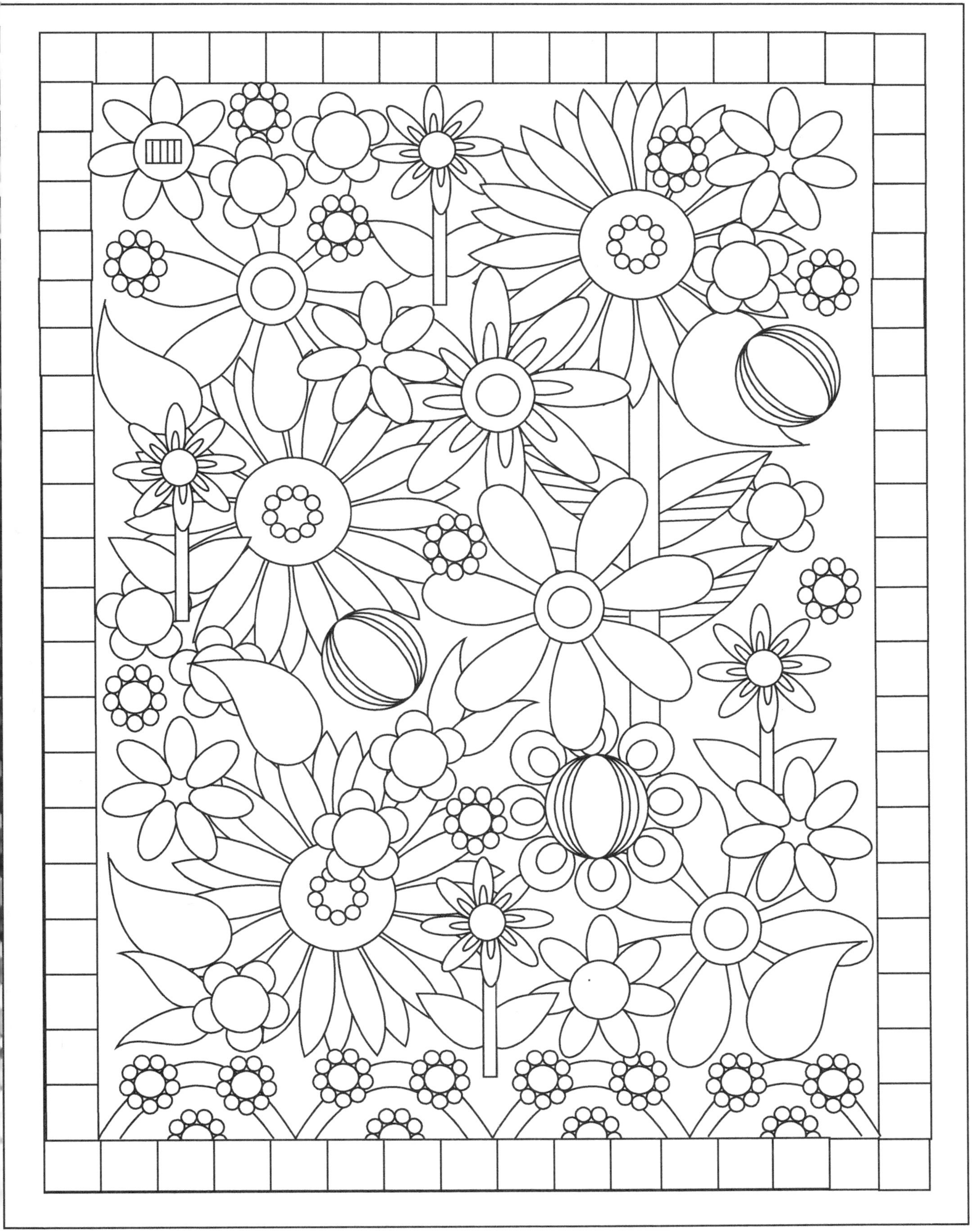

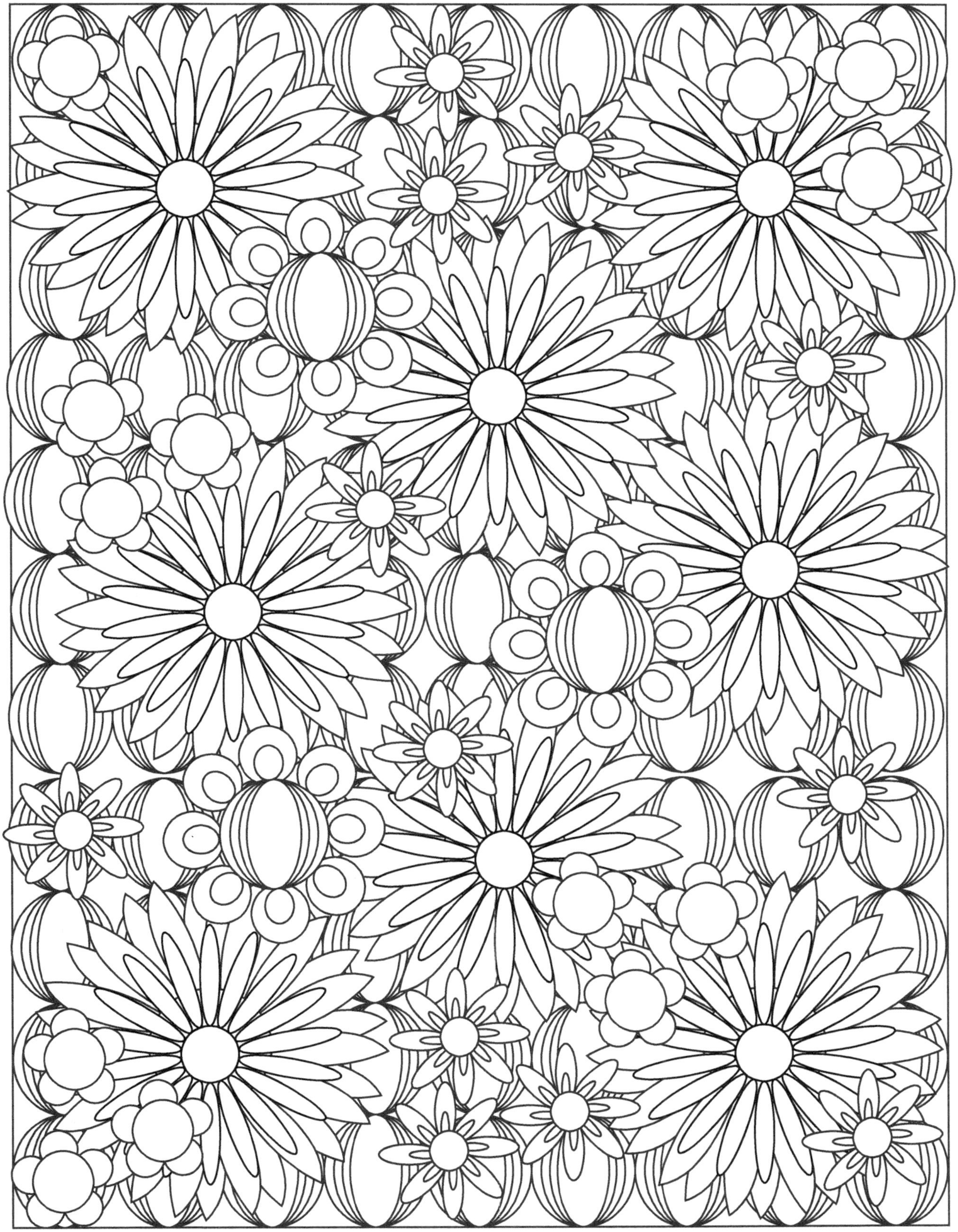

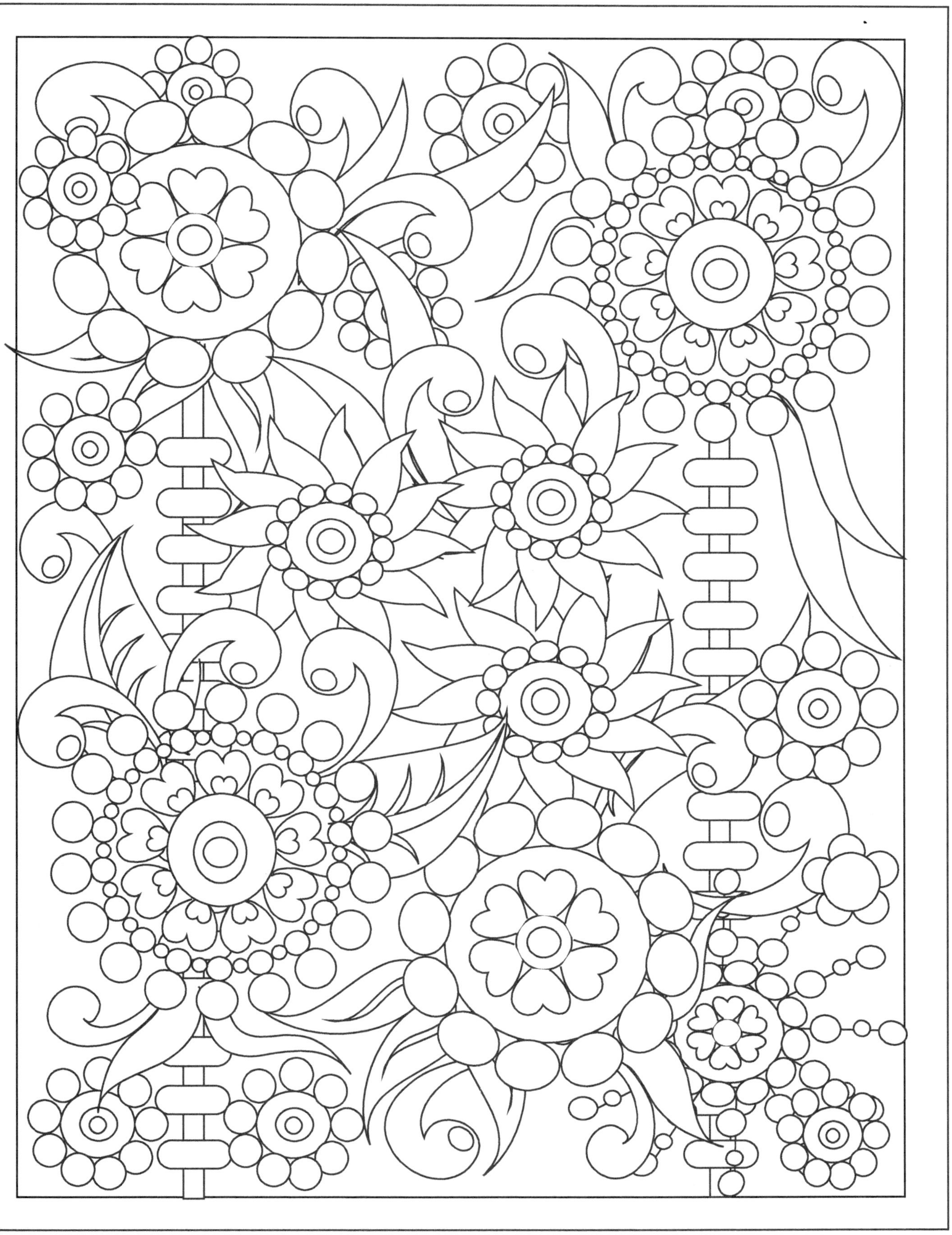

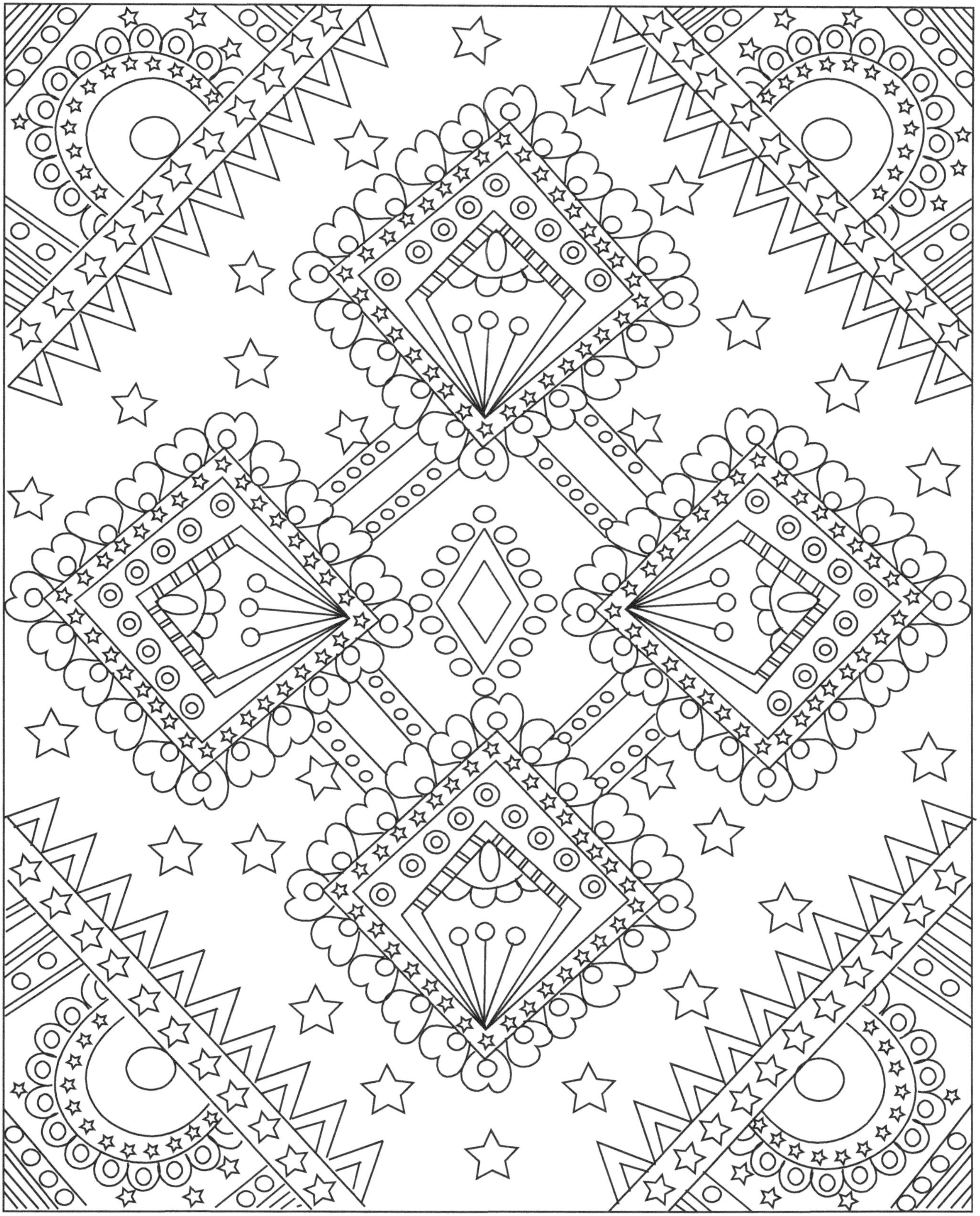

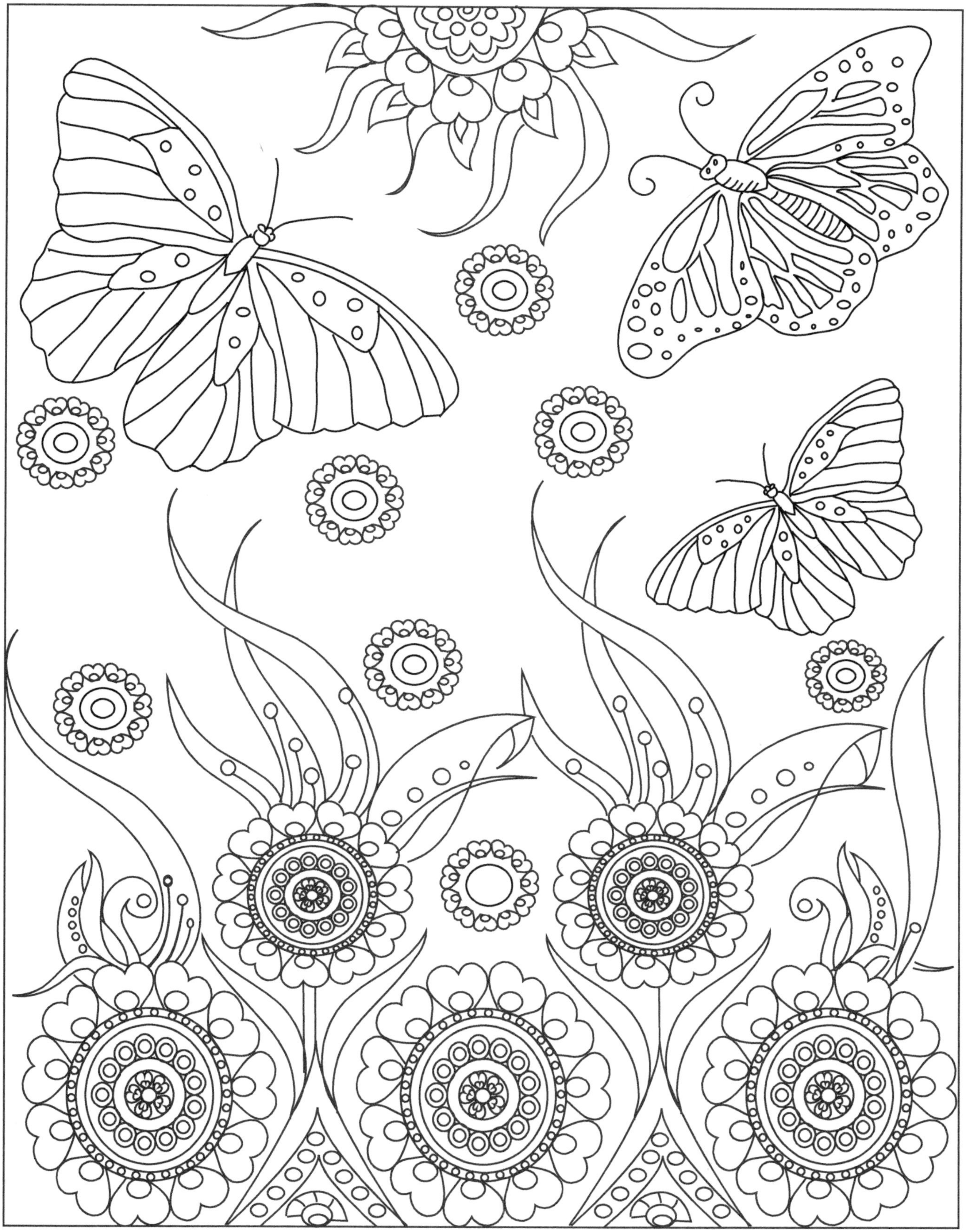

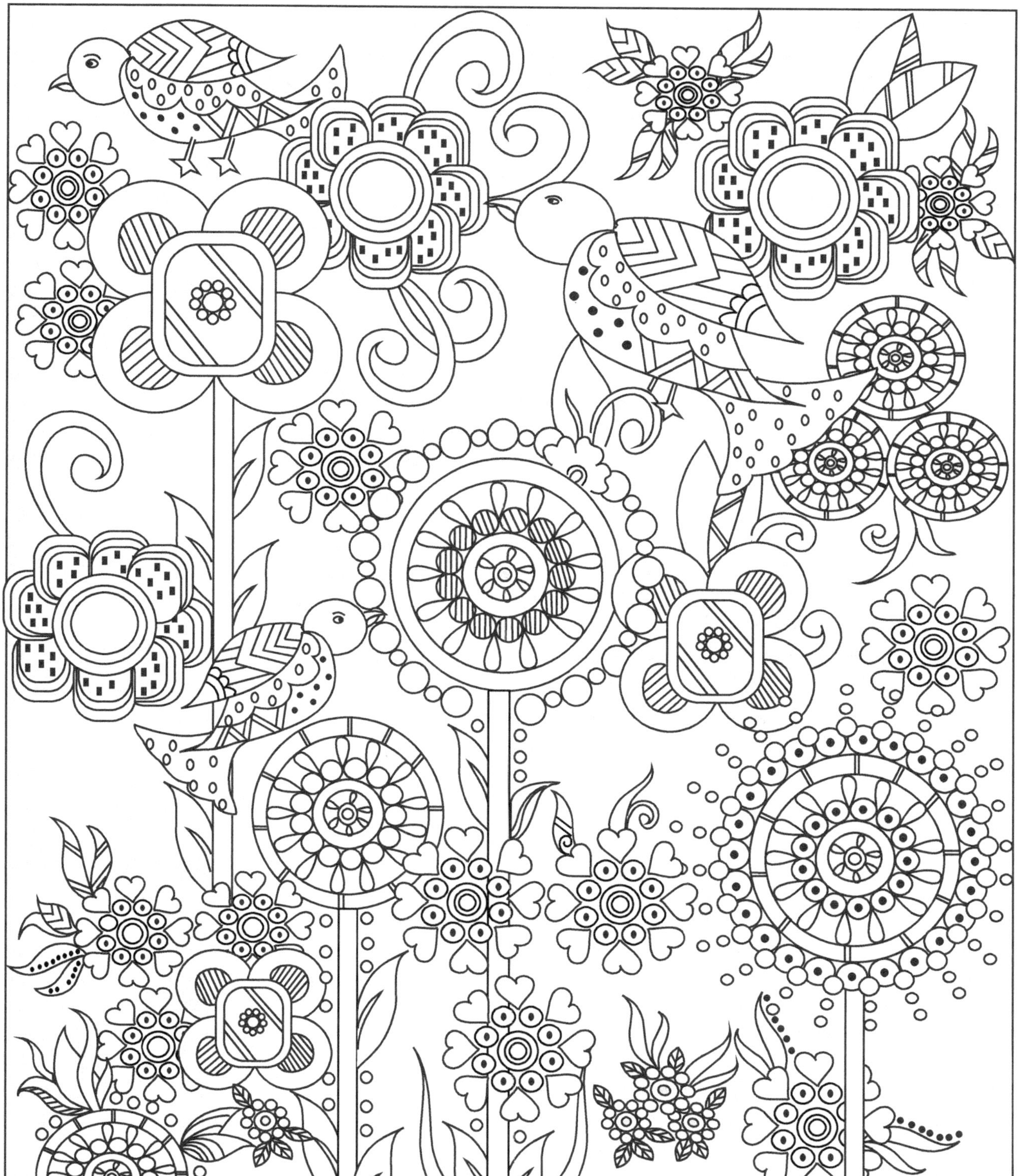

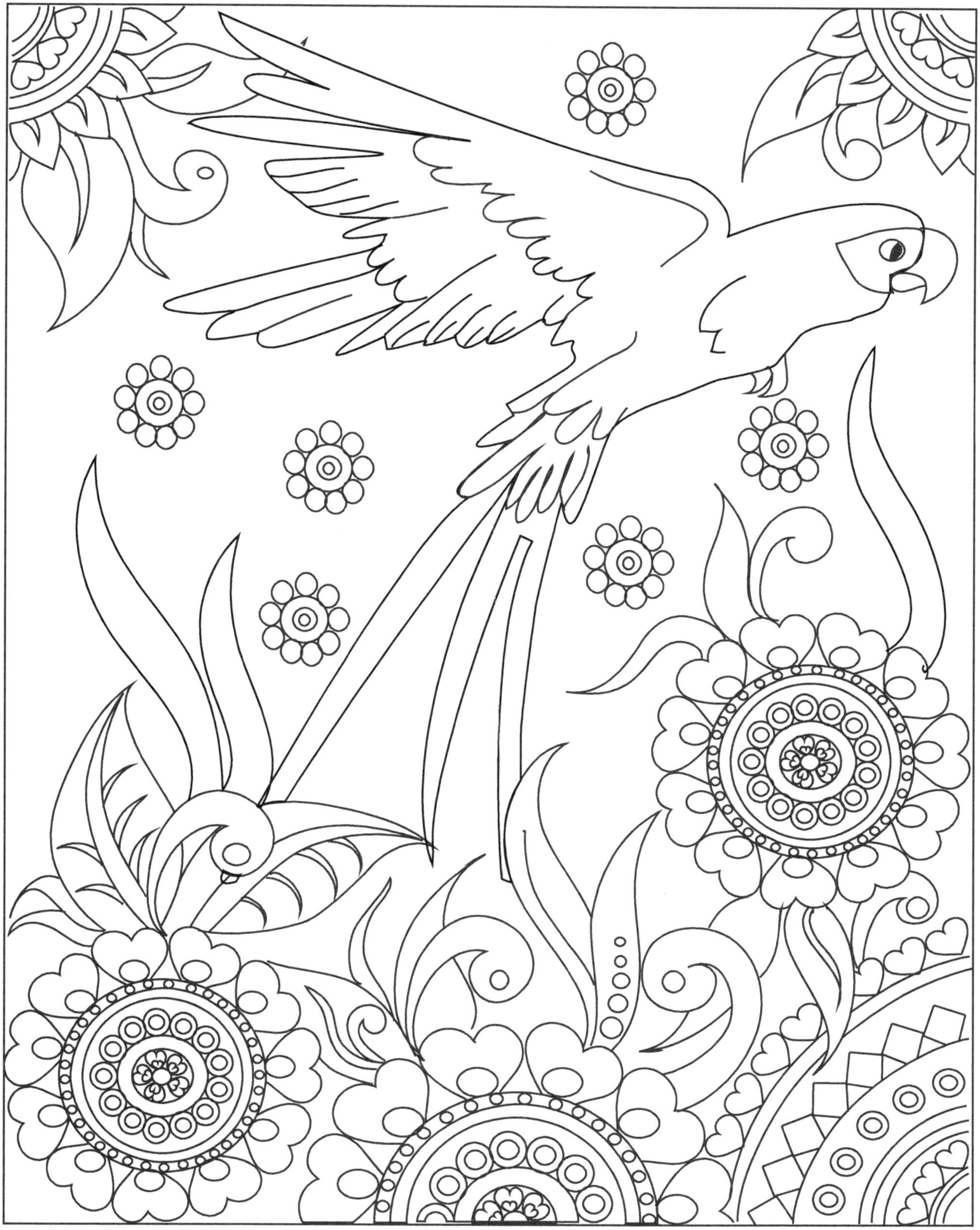

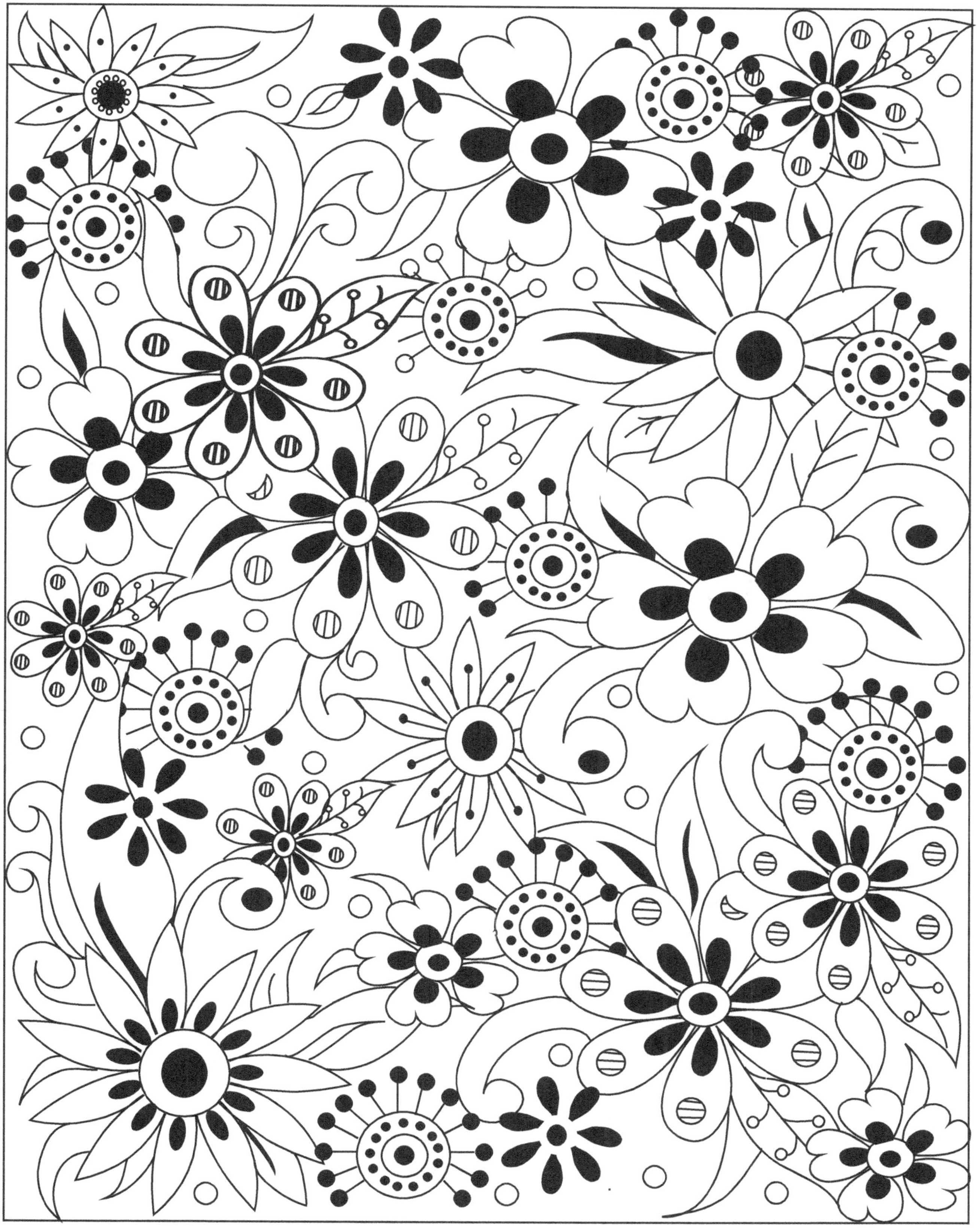

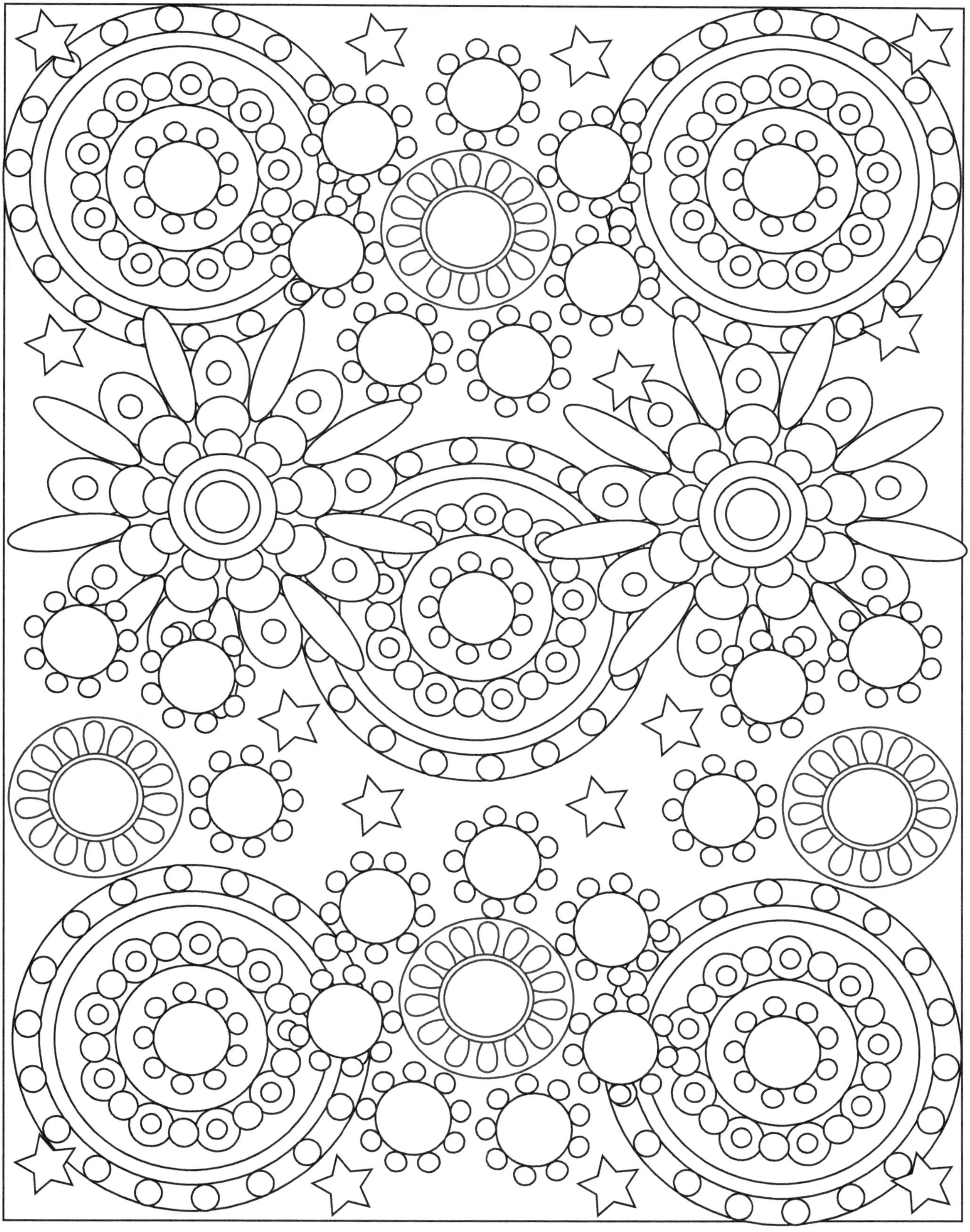

www.ingramcontent.com/pod-product-compliance
Lightning Source LLC
Chambersburg PA
CBHW062202220526
45470CB00009B/2900
*9781979477321*